# The Heart of Worship

## David Hadden

### in conversation with Christine Larkin

Freedom Publishing

A catalogue record for this book is available from the British Library

ISBN: 978-1908-154439

Cover design by Esther Kotecha, EKDesign
Typeset by Avocet Typeset, Somerton, Somerset, TA11 6RT
Printed and bound in the UK

# Table of Contents

# Dedication

To those who are leaders of worship,
and those who are leading the whole church
to become true worshippers, who might also
happen to be musicians and singers.

I fix my eyes
I fix my eyes
I fix my eyes on you

I set my gaze
I set my gaze
I set my gaze on you

For you are wonderful, so wonderful
You fill the expanse of my gaze
You are glorious, so glorious
How can my lips not praise?

© David Hadden

# Endorsements

David Hadden – there is no one better positioned to write a book on Worship (especially as it relates to the local church). He is a Worship Pastor, A Worship Leader, a prolific songwriter, an outstanding musician, a mentor to many, a lover of The Church. He is my friend. His passion for Christ has endured and survived many changing 'seasons of the soul'. He has remained undistracted in his calling. He has relentlessly pursued knowing the heart of God. I fully commend the works and life of this good man. What a blessing that he is sharing it in book form with us all.

Chris Bowater
Pastor and Worshipper


We consider Dave Hadden as a prophetic utterance from the mouth of God whose life points us to Jesus – he has inspired a generation of worshippers and lead worshippers with his incredible insight into how to establish the heart of worship in the local church globally but yet still there is a calls that echo in him for individuals to see and experience the simple Revelation of who Jesus is. We are grateful that God has blessed our generation with Dave a true father at the forefront of worship ministry around the globe!

Noel Robinson
Worship leader
Kingdom Worship Movement


David Hadden is a unique voice in modern church worship music. Kind, joyful, surprisingly hope bearing, and funny – David always catches people off guard and brings them quickly into the presence of God. David will have university classes enraptured with the kingdom message of his life and wit and spontaneous song-writing, then flip to a deep, reflective, half-a-century-of-ministry power flow. We love to see and hear David Hadden releasing God's creativity and sneaky joy in the congregants and musicians whenever we may.

Ken Steorts
President of Visible Music School
Memphis, USA


There are many worship mentors and also many worship pastors, but there are few who walk alongside you with fatherhood heart and enjoy your growth in the Lord. David Hadden, is a spiritual father, an encourager, a teacher and a good friend to me.

I encourage you to read this book and get nurtured from it, and I am sure you will hear David's fatherhood heart being released between the lines.

Roozbeh Najarnejad
Elam Ministries


I feel privileged to have David Hadden as a close friend and as a true brother in the Lord. He is also one of my 'go-to' people to ask the difficult questions and is always full of wise counsel and paternal encouragement which I guess makes him a father too! This ability stems from a rich journey as one of the pioneers of fresh worship expression birthed in the Charismatic Movement and his authority flows out of a challenging humility and the sense you get that he is totally at home in his own skin. This lack of insecurity means he is able to stand his ground on the issues of authenticity that keep worship presence-led but real and from the heart.

Richard Lewis
Worship Leader

# The Lion Roars

### Composer: David Hadden

There's a sound breaking out
From our hearts, from our mouths
It's a Lion's roar

There's a stirring inside
It's the sound of the Bride
It's a Lion's roar

There's a sound being birthed
That is filling the earth
It's a Lion's roar

Like a wave from the sea
It's the song of the free
It's a Lion's roar

The Lion roars
The Lion roars
The Lion roars

Though the darkness surrounds
For all those who've been bound
There's a Lion's roar

Breaking off every chain
That accompanies pain
There's a Lion's roar

Freedom
Freedom and Liberty
Freedom
Freedom and Liberty

The Lion roars..............

The Lion of the tribe of Judah
The Lion of the tribe of Judah
The Lion of the tribe of Judah
Has triumphed

We say, Yes, Lord.  X3

## Introduction

# God has given me a voice

When we were living in St Louis, I was visiting a congregation and the Sunday morning speaker was a Bible student from Zambia. He spoke one sentence that really stuck with me: 'you have a voice into the world that you live in'. The truth and the power of those words really sank into my heart and I have used that sentence over the years and because I am involved in the world of worship God has given me a voice into that world that I live in.

And whatever world you live in, God has given you a voice into your world.

> **You have a voice into the world that you live in.**

The implication is that the world we live in can receive the voice of heaven through us. Over the years the Lord has blessed me and allowed me to do that, speaking into worship conferences, worship teams, leaders, musicians, singers, and songwriters sharing some of the heart foundations and revelations that I have had, which then becomes their revelation applied to their own lives.

In Matthew 28 Jesus said to His disciples 'all authority in heaven and earth has been given to me, therefore go in my authority and make disciples. Now what I skilfully do with worship leaders and songwriters is to share the heart of what God has given me and that has become their foundation from which to work.

## Chapter 1

# First Mention of Music

There's a principle in scripture of first mention, where a word or a phrase or a concept is mentioned for the first time it has an extra significance, a special importance and when we delve into that we can learn a lot about that word, that idea, that thought, as we allow it to filter into our lives and hearts. There is a power in it and if we can turn that key there is power available.

The first one I want to look at is the first mention of music in the Scriptures and we find it in Genesis 4:19-21 Lamech married two women, one Adah and one Zillah. Adah gave birth to Jabal, who was the father of those who live in tents and raise livestock. His brother's name was Jubal and he was the father of those who play stringed instruments and pipes.

> *Genesis 4:21 Jubal, the father of those who played stringed instruments and pipes*

I read that a number of years ago and researched it. It fascinated me in an investigative way as I wanted to find out more about this person Jubal. Of course, Jubal is a derivative of Jubilee which speaks a lot about the year of Jubilee, freedom etc. But that is another subject. When I looked at Jubal, I realised that he was a son, a bother and a father. What I discovered here was the context of multigenerational continuity and relational connection.

His father had two sons and both had an anointing and both were different. As we know all our children are different. One gifted in one direction and one in another. The brother Jubal who was gifted in music also became a father. Obviously, he was the first of many and that gave him the God-given right to set the tone for everything that was to follow. It mentions in Genesis 4:21 that he was the father of all who play stringed instruments and pipes (NIV). Other versions mention different instruments. He is the spiritual father of all instrument players. Well that is very nice and I am thrilled about that but what does it mean for me as a musician living today? I started to do some delving into the name of Jubal and I looked at the meaning of his name and was flabbergasted. His name means to flow like a river. Jubal, who flowed like a river is the father of all who play instruments. Therefore, I believe all musicians should play like their father and play like a flowing river. Sometimes a river flows gently and sometimes it is really violent in its flowing. Both fast and slow areas of running water can occur. The potential of being able to bring in different styles of music even in the same piece is infinitesimal. The interesting thing is that a river charts its course by its God-made banks and it may turn and weave. We used to live in St Louis by the Mississippi river and that river meanders from side to side, not just in a straight line. It meanders, impacting twice or three times as much of the land than if it was straight. If it ran in a straight line it would be like a canal and canals are man-made, whereas rivers are God-made.

> **The deeper a river the deeper the flow. So, it is with our music.**

I don't mind canals but I would rather be on a river that is a living entity that flows. Rivers ebb and flow and our worship should have a flow and progression to it the deeper we get. The deeper a river goes the deeper the flow, so should our music be. In a worship service, as people call it, instead of playing a song and stopping why not just keep it going? No river has a break to stop flowing. No river ever does that, it just keeps on going.

To play a song is easy, to join two songs together is much more difficult. Too many people practice what happens in the songs but they don't practice what happens in between the songs, i.e. the flow section. The learning and practice of songs should be done by every musician in the quietness of their home. Then before a public meeting on Sunday morning they should run through sections of the song, but then practice the bridging; the gaps between the songs. They are important parts of our meeting. A fifteen second time period can determine what happens subsequently in the meeting. It can release a prophetic environment and the power of entering into a new song. What often happens is the song finishes and everybody waits for what is coming next, or they sit down, or they look to the band. Instead of engaging in the flow of the river, they engage in a spectator sport of a "musical performance."

We need to practice flowing between one song and another. Learn how to transpose into different keys and how to play songs in different keys. We, as musicians in the church, need to learn these tools so we can use them as we need to. To keep the flow going, when one song finishes, you need to keep the music playing until you are ready to go into the next song. Jubal can speak to us today to mean that we have the opportunity to cause a meeting, that we are in, to have a flow. It is important for musicians today, who are used to the concert style, to learn how to keep the flow going. In a secular context the concert style is fine but in a worship context the flow must keep going.

For example, if you take the song 'How Great is our God' in A. When you come to the end of the song don't finish it but keep repeating the A chord and think ahead to what you know might come next. That will determine what you do in the bridge section. You might go to a next song in D Major. Then you would move from A to D, A to D, A to D, then G A to D without batting an eyelid. It's simple! That's an easy example of how to transition from one key into the next one, and prepare for what is coming next. A trained musician should be able to think about something else when they are playing something. If you can't that is something you need to practice. You learn how to think about the next song while playing the current one and plan for it, the timing, the key signature.

A friend of mine told me that practice for a musician is very interesting. He said amateur musicians' practice until they can play it correctly where professional musicians practice until they can't get it wrong. Practice transitions if you know the songs as they are vital to your ability to flow between songs in a meeting.

> *Amateur musicians' practice until they can play it correctly. Professional musicians' practice until they can't get it wrong.*

In music the theoretical and practical are vital. When I was being trained as a pianist, I had to learn the theory to understand the application of the practical. When I was having my piano lessons, occasionally I would cut corners in the music and play the "chords" and the melody. This of course was not written in the music and my piano teacher would stop me and say I wasn't playing the music correctly. I would say I am playing the chords and she would say 'what chords'? At that moment I realised that I was seeing some musical stuff that my teacher couldn't see. My piano teacher could still teach me practically, but not in this new way of playing that I was beginning to understand. In my own teaching of others, it's about teaching them to understand the theory in the music, and to help them move from that first rung of the ladder of understanding to the next rung, and so on.

*That sounds OK if you are the worship leader but what about the other musicians? How would they know? Would everyone on the platform usually know the list of songs?*

If there is a song list, they would all know and they could practice the transitions assuming they had time to do that and not just before the meeting. Normally there is a mid-week practice where we could sort out some of that technical stuff. **However, the midweek rehearsal should never take the place of personal practice and learning.**

Transition points need to be taught and practised. Occasionally, if I am leading from the keyboard alongside another worship leader, one of the Church leaders may come and request we sing a certain song. This means not only have I got to sing and play the song we are currently singing, whilst leading the team, I also have to

20

listen to the leader, respond to them by nodding, while thinking how that song goes, what key it is in and then at the appointed time move from song one to song two. A tall order you may say!! When I first started to do this, it was a disaster! Now having practised it, I can do it, even if someone is speaking in my ear while I am playing.

PRACTICE! PRACTICE! PRACTICE!

Once you have learnt it – teach someone else!

NB – we must always remember that our worship is unto the Lord. He should be our primary focus. Not the song list!

# There's no veil any longer

## Composer: David Hadden

There's no veil any longer
To separate the Church
From the presence of the Lord
There's no veil any longer
We enter with sincere and grateful hearts

Lord we come into your courts
With a sacrifice of praise
Lord, we come in confidence
With a sacrifice of praise
Maker of all heaven and earth
We are wonderfully made
Lord of all the universe
We are gloriously saved

Boldly we approach the throne
We are yours, and not our own
For who you are, for what you've done
We worship you.

## Chapter 2

# First Mention of Worship

> *Genesis 22:2 Abraham take your son, your only son, whom you love and go to the region of Moriah and sacrifice him there.*

*We have covered the first mention of music. What other first mentions are there?*

The first mention of worship in the Bible had nothing to do with singing songs or playing instruments. In Genesis 22 it says 'some time later God tested Abraham and He said to him, Abraham, take your son, your only son, whom you love and go to the region of Moriah and sacrifice him there.

The response of Abraham in verse 3 was that early the next morning they set off on a journey to the place God had said. The journey took three days and no doubt Isaac was asking his Dad questions like 'Are we there yet?', 'What time's lunch?', etc. All the kind of things boys ask their Dads.

When they reached the place, Abraham told the servants to wait while he went ahead with Isaac to 'worship.' This is the first time the word worship appears in scripture. Abraham didn't take a guitar, keyboard, drum kit or iPad. He took the wood, a blazing torch for the fire and a knife! I am sure there is a lot of significance in those three things, but I am not going to talk about that here. The concept that I want to communicate is that worship is intrinsically about sacrifice and obedience, not about the singing of slow songs. A worshipful lifestyle is like Abraham saying "YES" to God and getting up early to do what God has asked him to do.

In the church today, you go to a meeting and the worship leader stands at the front and the band strikes up and a time of worship begins. I believe the worship should never have stopped since the last time the Church gathered. Worship doesn't mean playing or singing songs. It is a heart issue that rolls on throughout lives of obedience and sacrifice.

If we look into Romans 12:1 we read 'I urge you in view of God's mercy to offer your bodies as a living sacrifice holy and pleasing to God, this is true and proper worship. In verse 2 it says, 'Do not conform to the pattern of the world but be transformed by the renewing of your mind'. God is saying don't copy the world but run with the true pattern from heaven and follow that.

### How would you advise a church on having a worship team?

I am not too keen on the title 'worship team' because really everyone in the congregation should be the "worship team." I have often asked people in church to put their hands up if they are on the worship team. Normally, only the musicians and singers put their hands up! Then I ask the rest of the congregation why they didn't respond! You see – perception of who God has made us to be is not fully understood by the Bride! And sometimes, it is easier to get on to God's worship team, than the "actual" worship team in some churches.

Let me tell you – it is easy to get on God's worship team – we just have to be worshippers!

Worshippers are those who are willing to lay down their lives in obedience to God. That really is the heart of a true worshipper. It's not a "one-off gig!"

# It is you and you alone

Composer: David Hadden

It is you and you alone
That I long for
That I hope for
It is you and you alone
That satisfies my soul

It's not the gift
It's not the call
It's you my all in all
It's not the joy
It's not the peace
It's you that must increase
It is you and you alone
That satisfies my soul

# Chapter 3

# Trained and Skilled

> *1 Chronicles 25:27 – Along with their relatives – all of them trained and skilled in music for the Lord – they numbered 288*

In this verse we can see that the relational context was important as part of their engagement in music for the Lord. The number 288 represented 24 hours of the day and 12 musicians. This is the concept of round the clock adoration and response to the Lord. It says along with their relatives. Relatives are generally those who you are close too, share your life with. I would suggest in our worship teams today that it is important to share life together. The members of the team having connection, showing interest in each other. It is a two-way relationship. This is a learning journey I have had to make over the years. When I first started, I had no relationship with my team and I became convicted by God to take responsibility for them and to be involved in their lives. I now try to do that with every person on my team and my attitude to them changed. **I need to be personable.**

The next part of the verse is to ensure all the team are trained and skilled in music.

**Do you mean they should keep having music lessons?**

Sometimes it is needed but they need to learn from someone who will tell them what is not right and not just praise them. Being trained and being skilled are two completely different things. When I was learning to play the piano, my teacher trained me in how to technically play the music. Everyone on the team should have a teacher. You can go on YouTube and learn from that or you might want a 1:1 teacher. Everyone needs to be pressing in further to improve through practice or learning new techniques.

Being trained – the how to's!

Being Skilled – understanding the where, the why and the when!

**Are you saying that part of your worship is to always seek to give your best to the Lord and not just about improving your ability?**

Absolutely. We never stop learning at whatever age we are at. Even at my age I am on a quest to learn more. Training for musicians is different from training for a singer. Almost everyone has an accent when they sing. I have learnt that the words of a song are really important and I must convey every word of the song to a congregation to help them to join in. If I am sloppy and lazy in my diction, no-one will understand me. I am always training my team in their diction with a clear start and end. You can still have an accent but it must be clear and crisp in delivery. Training means learning to improve. The skill element is where you can do it well all the time. There is also a need of training for multiple singers together. That is another whole level of skill to develop, ensuring they start and end all lyrics at the same time. PRO-NUN-C-IA-TION!

I am starting to train our worship team in the difference between listening and hearing. I get them all to listen during the week and when we come together to practice, they will all be singing differently. That shows that they are hearing it but not really listening. Our singers must have joined up approach, as opposed to a group of individuals. Synchronised singing, is far better than everybody doing their own thing! The skillful side for a musician is knowing when to change up to a faster tempo or slow down in a free flow worship context. Then the musician and the singer can enter into a greater intensity of worship. I remember listening to an orchestral conductor judging Young Musician of the Year. The interviewer asked what she was listening for and she said all of them can play but I am listening for how they play. Because how they play marks them out from the others and how they make the music live. For me as a worship team leader I am looking for people who make the music come alive when they play. That is the difference from being trained and being skilled.

# Chapter 4

# Together With

> *1 Chronicles 25:1 – David, together with the commanders of the army set apart some of the sons of Asaph, Heman and Jeduthun for the ministry of prophesying, accompanied by harps, lyres and cymbals.*

In 1 Chronicles 25 the first eight verses are a great teaching tool, a revelation tool, for not only the development and training of worship teams but churches and ministries. I want to talk about David who was a king, worshipper, soldier, father etc. Verse 1 begins with the phrase 'David, together with'. This is an important key for us. You would think a king would be separate, aloof, yet David was not that kind of person. He was 'connected' as opposed to disconnected and that is a very important lesson to us. We need to be people who are connected to one another. When we are disconnected, we can have a "great ministry," but lack the benefit of others in terms of their input, or help, or insight. When you are connected you might not have a ministry but you are loved and people connect with you and will share their heart with you.

### David did that.

Yes, he did when he had to. In this chapter it is about David being with the commanders of the army. You might say, what have the commanders of the army to do with being a worship team. Well if you can visualise what qualities and characters commanders would carry you can see why David wanted to connect with them. Commanders need to be seers from a long way off and to be able to observe situations, quantify what needs to be done and set long and short-term vision. Here we have the king together with the brave, fearless, commanders who could step into a situation where all the odds were against them. The modern-day portrayal of that would be a seer or a prophet – David together with the prophet and apostolic set apart a team. If a worship leader thinks they are qualified to 'choose' a worship team, dream on. I have tried it and it doesn't work!

### Why doesn't it work?

Because you can't see in the way an apostolic or prophet seer can. For years now I have made it a practice to share with the Church leadership team about who to have on the worship team. I would let them know who I was thinking of having on the team and asking the leaders how they feel about having them function. The leader might say that it isn't appropriate, or, it is OK to go ahead. An example is that there may be personal or character issues which need to be addressed by the leadership. This of course needs doing. This practice is extremely positive, as it has the person's freedom in view. It is also to cover the person to ensure they aren't exposed prematurely, and to cover myself. It is my responsibility to be accountable to the Leadership.

There is a sense of the apostolic and the prophetic flowing together in decision making as worship is so important in the church.

*You have explained how the church leadership might be involved but how does the prophetic link to worship leading? How would the prophetic giftings work alongside the worship?*

The prophetic can actually take time to pray into what is happening and prophesy over the worship team. We have the prayer group to come into the worship team to pray and prophesy over them which is just as important as the practical element. If you make the worship purely practical, they will function in a very practical way and it will all be nicely packaged.

But we want to have prophetic people, who hear from the Spirit, speak into us and this is good, as it means a **reliance on God rather than on practical gifting**. Even on Sunday the worship operates alongside the moving of the Spirit and if the prophetic voice has something to bring, we, as worship leaders and teams, must submit ourselves to that anointing even if we are in the middle of a song. The word of God needs to be released and it is our responsibility to respond to what the Lord is saying, rather than just singing another song! **It's a really important lesson for churches**.

I remember one time a friend of mine asked me to play keyboard in his church for a weekend of meetings. I travelled down and the band was set up on the platform and for two hours we rehearsed every single song from the count in to the count out. At the end I asked my friend, who was leading the worship, if the rest of his team knew all the songs. He said that they did. I asked why he was spending two hours going over things they already knew. I suggested he should spend time going through the difficult parts of the songs but then spend time over coffee, fellowshipping with the worship team and leaders. He said that wasn't how they did things! I thought that was very sad. I know some musicians like to practice over and over, but I prefer to just focus on what is really needed and spend time with the team.

Catching the heart of the Prophetic is vitally important and it all begins with listening.

*What about the need for the 'anointing' in a worship team context? Not everybody will be flowing in the same way.*

The scripture says the anointing breaks the yoke of slavery. There are times and moments when you will be engaging in worship and then suddenly there is a prophetic word or a song released and the atmosphere changes. We need to be ready for this!

**When he walks into the room, everything changes!**

You will find the worship then will move differently. Those who see and hear, need to put their spiritual antenna up in the meeting. I remember when we were back in Bradford at the end of the 1980s, we were enjoying a season of high praise. I had never heard anything like it. It just went on and on in the meeting. Bryn Jones came up to preach and we were in a realm of high praise in the Spirit and the whole congregation were engaged. I watched Bryn with his hands lifted up worshipping, and it was like a bag of sand hit him in the stomach and he crashed to the floor. In the Spirit, of course!! The Church leader, Paul Scanlon was leading the meeting. Having seen what happened, he then encouraged us to press on in praise. The meeting moved to a whole new level. When moments like these come, they are opportunities to go with the flow. Alternatively, we can press on with the programme! It takes courage as a leader to go with the flow of the Spirit.

When a leadership team work in tandem, together with heaven's perspective, new heights, depths and perspectives of the Spirit can be reached. In the same way, a worship team leader needs to teach his team how to tap into heaven's realm in order that they can learn to identify who is carrying the anointing to play or sing spontaneously and freshly. Then they need to know to release that person by creating space for them and letting creativity flow. It would be ideal that the team all know each other so well that they can move as one. If I sense something needs to be released and I am not the one with the anointing, but someone else is, then I will signal them to release them. Watch others who have responsibility for the meeting and work in tandem with them.

### How does someone who is leading the meeting manage the worship leader when it is time to transition but they don't know how to stop the musician?

There has to be an honouring and serving of one another. If you have a song list it is easy and everyone knows what is happening. We don't want that! We want to be led by the Spirit and for everyone to be open to releasing the flow of the river, the word of knowledge or prophetic words. The congregation will know when there is a transition and they will be looking for the one who will release according to the Spirit. Once again, it is all about relationship. A "together with" relationship. The scenario can be risky and challenging, but it is very exciting! We are after relational worship and relational church. As a worship leader, I must be aware of what is happening in any meeting and be willing to pause my plan for another.

*How would you speak to the tendency to be a 'lone ranger' in ministry – the opposite of 'together with'?*

God wants us to have healed hearts where we connect to one another. If the worship leader is a lone ranger, they should be helped by Church leadership before being released to that position. Everyone needs to develop relational teams, not those who have "lone ranger" tendencies, leading them out of that position, and using language of 'we' and not 'I'. Language is extremely powerful in how we lead teams and it is part of discipling to use the language of relationship. That's why language in our songs is powerful. Some songs which are *'I'* focused need to be changed to *'we'*. Not all of them of course. We need to be aware that corporate songs, to have a corporate response, need to have 'we' statements. Of course, technically you can do that but legally you can't change someone else's song. And that is another story!

We also need to teach and train our songwriters, who are penning new material to make it corporate. Please!!

*The person projecting the words on the screen is part of the 'together with' in worship teams. How do you include the technical people as part of the team?*

What we are doing in Leicester is to ensure the words are in the computer days before the meeting, checking for spellings and punctuation. The technical people are as much part of the team and they should at least be there for sound checks to prepare for all the songs which we might pick. The people doing this very important job may also need to be available to come to Worship Team meetings for training. Communication with all the team during the meeting is paramount for a worship team leader. The leader needs to sing and think ahead, and at the same time let the person on the projector know if you are going to change a verse.

## Chapter 5

# Set Apart

> *1 Chronicles 25:1 – David, together with the commanders of the army set apart some of the sons of Asaph, Heman and Jeduthun for the ministry of prophesying, accompanied by harps, lyres and cymbals.*

David and his commanders set apart for the ministry of prophesying <u>accompanied</u> by musical instruments. Our musicians and singers are not just those who can "carry" a song. There has to be an element of the prophetic in them. The ability to respond to the prophetic, or the ability to move in a prophetic mantle. Also, our worship must be prophetic too. It must carry the DNA of heaven, carry responsiveness to heaven. The instruments accompany the prophetic, whether it is for a song or a spontaneous contribution. Not many people who are classically trained on an instrument are taught how to accompany. When you are trained it is to perform. However, what the scripture is saying here is that musicians are there to accompany, and how you play when you accompany is completely different from how you would play when you are performing. There are different ways to play and sing a song. You can play a song for one person but when the congregation are singing the worship leaders are accompanying.

When I was performing my exam pieces, I was drawing the attention of the examiner to me. As an accompanist, I must play in a way that draws attention to God, and to the lyrics of a song, or to the Word that is being released in that prophetic moment. As musicians it is our role to enhance the song by how we play. Please don't get in the way! Don't be so loud that no-one can hear, or sing the words, and don't show off your skilfulness on your instrument. Simplify what you play to draw the listeners ear to where it needs to be. **Play in such a way that enhances the power of the moment.**

By now we should have learnt that there are different ways to play and sing a song. Whoever our audience is, remember that Heaven is always watching and listening.

### *Where does the prophetic come in?*

The musicians are part of the prophetic. If you were giving a word, I would play very simply behind you to accompany what you are saying. The attention must not be on me, but to draw attention to what the Lord is saying through the prophetic word. I would want everyone's attention to be on the word and to enhance what you are saying while I play. I have to practice this constantly!

*I do love it when there is that 'wash' of sound as I am prophesying. I find it actually adds to what I am saying by the Spirit of God encouraging me through the wash of sound accompanying the prophetic word. It is almost like they are one and the same.*

Absolutely. I am looking to undergird what is being released. Again, in this scripture it says 'accompanied by harps, lyres and cymbals'. Generally, when someone prophesies it will be a keyboard playing. It is time to train our teams for everyone to be able to keep playing during a prophesy but sympathetic to what is being brought prophetically.

*That excites me. I know that if there was a 'team' of people all flowing when I am prophesying that it would move me up a level in the release of the word, assuming they were actually flowing in the Spirit!*

The interesting thing is, for the musicians, they not only have to listen to what they have to play but they also need to listen to the word, to be able to really hear the word and flow with it. They mustn't play too loud above the word, but accompany the prophetic, and when the Spirit moves it is an atmosphere shifter. If you were prophesying and I was playing I might just hold a chord and then when you shifted into another gear in what you were bringing, I would shift to a different chord. There is this 'together with' for the prophetic and the worship rather than you bring a word on your own.

There is one word in this verse which is very interesting. It says David set apart 'some' of the sons. Why? Does it mean that some weren't set apart? If so, why? My thoughts are that some were gifted and anointed in musicianship and some were not – like Jabal and Jubal. Jabal was a farmer and Jubal was a musician, each with different anointings.

Over in 1 Chronicles 25 again, another interesting point is that Asaph wasn't just a leader of musicians, he was a gatherer of people. That is what his name means. Some leaders will be gatherers. The next man, Heman, means 'faithful father'. There you have a gatherer working alongside a faithful father. Then you have the third man, Jeduthun, means to give thanks and praise. This powerful threesome comprised of a gatherer, a faithful father, and a giver of thanks and praise. When each were operating in their function that is what they reproduced corporately. Our worship teams require their leaders to be gatherers, mothers and father and releasers of thanks and praise.

*Another aspect of 'together with' for worship teams is how they engage relationally with the wider church body outside of that gifting, especially if they are busy with music practice during the week and getting to the meeting early to set up.*

I make it a point on a Sunday to move out and engage with the congregation before the meeting, chatting to them and finding out how they are doing. It is really important to be together with the wider congregation. I used to be busy sorting out my instruments and equipment but now I realise it is important to interact with others outside of the worship team. I would sometimes say to my team at the end of the meeting they are not to touch their instruments for ten minutes but to go out and talk to the congregation, getting to know them. Of course, this is a journey for us all!

# God is looking

## Composer: David Hadden

God is looking for a people
Who will worship him in Sprirt and in truth
He is calling for a nation
To be hol-y

And we will be the people
You are looking for
We will be your children
And you our God
Seeking first your kingdom
Walking in your will
We'll be faithful, Lord

God is seeking a generation
Of those who are devoted to his will
And he is calling for this nation
To be holy

Chapter 6

# Worship leading in different settings

*You mention worship is not just something we do in church. Obviously, we all have personal worship times of connection with the Lord. What other ways can we worship?*

## At home

If we can understand that worship is much more than playing and singing songs, then there is a chance that we will be able to live our lives throughout the week as worshippers. Learning to lay down our lives for others. **Romans 12:1 – Offer your bodies and a living sacrifice, holy and pleasing to God.**

Should you happen to be a worship leader in a public setting you are still a worship leader at home. The church needs mothers and fathers in worship leading. At home you have to carry the heart of a worship leader. Rather than gather the family around your instrument to sing, be real and normal as possible, loving your family, a life given over to God. If you are as real as possible at home when you are leading a meeting in church you will be real and normal as well. That will be helpful and encouraging to the team and the congregation. Please don't make it about you. The underlying subtitle of this chapter is **honour**. God has honoured me and I need to honour my family, my neighbours, my work colleagues, the local church, the congregation, the Church leadership team and the worship team I am in. And if I happen to be somewhere else I must honour the people whose church I am visiting!

The key message is leading by example of being a servant rather than making demands. When you go to a larger setting, such as a conference, **don't go to be seen but to serve**. Sometimes I purposefully stand at the side to see the congregation and not to be the focal point of the whole worship.

I've seen both men and women worship leaders who act like prima donnas! Don't do it! Just be yourself and draw people's attention and focus on Jesus! If you are flamboyant that's fine, but if quiet be yourself but be aware you are ushering in an atmosphere for a corporate experience. In big settings whenever I have led large conferences, I always ask those who carry responsibility for the meeting to help me, and if they have something to bring by way of a contribution, they will not be "Stepping on my toes" by releasing what they have. After all, this is not "my meeting!"

# Big events/Conferences

*What are the challenges when leading outside your home church? How would someone know if they are ready for a bigger context?*

I believe the way we prepare for a bigger context, is to show ourselves faithful at home. Be a humble servant, and a blessing to whoever you are with. **Learn to serve another person's vision before you run with your own!**

In a big event, five hundred plus people, it is really the same – getting to know the worship team, the Church leaders, the congregation etc. Basically, be a people's person! On occasion the main leader may be absent for some reason – it is then the responsibility of the Church leadership team to own the responsibility for that meeting. Sometimes if the main worship leader is struggling, it is right for leadership to step in and cover their back, maybe taking the microphone, supporting them. There should be a relationship with the Church leadership which is based on honour and respect. The worship leader should make time to build relationships with the team, getting to know them, caring about them.

If you hold on to the leadership with clasped fists you will be disappointed. If you hold it with open hands you won't be disappointed.

# Visiting other churches

*I am sometimes asked to speak in other churches and it can be quite challenging if I am unfamiliar with their culture or practice. It must be even harder for a worship leader to go into a different church. What is your experience?*

If I am going to another church to lead worship my priority is to find out what they sing and help the congregation to enter into worship by singing some of the songs that they are used to singing, even if it doesn't fully fit the flow of what I planned. It is important for me to honour them as opposed to expect them to honour me. It is an honour to be invited and my honour is to serve them. I went to a church one time and the leader told me to do whatever I want. I said I wouldn't do that as it is their church not mine, their congregation not mine and I am there to serve them. It all goes back to right relationship. For me to be invited somewhere and just do my own thing is massively short-sighted because all I am doing is promoting myself when my role is to promote Jesus with the congregation.

## Chapter 7

# And finally....

This book is entitled after one of the most influential of worship songs.

> I'm coming back to the heart of worship
> And it's all about you
> It's all about you, Jesus
> I'm sorry Lord, for the thing I've made it
> When it's all about you
> It's all about you, Jesus
>
> Written by Matt Redman

The heart of this book, and the heart of our worship, must be focused into our revelation of King Jesus on the Throne of Heaven, and then on to the implications of the outworking of that into our world. It is with this in view that we embark upon a life calling into worship. After all, God is looking for worshippers.

*Yet a time is coming and has now come when the true worshippers will worship the Father in spirit and truth, for they are the kind of worshippers the Father seeks. God is spirit and his worshippers must worship in spirit and in truth.* John 4:23

The responsibility lies with us. We are those people that God is speaking of. He is looking and searching for those who will give themselves to a life of worship. To live a life that honours God and is devoted to fixing their eyes on him above all others.

A number of years ago I wrote a song called: Living under the shadow of his wing. The song is a very activating as it begins with the word – "living." It is a daily devotion and action that focuses our attention on heaven, rather than on earth. Other key words in the song are "standing," "bowed," "voices joined together," "heart to heart," and "soaring." These words and phrases are not passive, but active. They are both personal and corporate.

My prayer is that the heart of these lyrics, and this includes Matt's lyrics, will become foundational in our lives. Lives fixed and focused on Heaven. Receiving love, grace, health, vision and all that Heaven has to give. Of course, all of those benefits come from heaven, but the release of these require us to first to give ourselves unreservedly to the Lord.

Our journey into discovering the heart of worship is a lifetime pursuit. As we give ourselves unreservedly to pursuing the vision and allow God to take us by the hand and lead us deeper into it. I remember when I was in my twenties thinking if I would still be doing this when I was in my sixties? Well, yes, I am. I am so grateful for the way that God has cared for us as a family and led us on this adventure.

When you embark on an adventure not every road ahead is straight and flat! Life is filled with challenges, successes and failures. And unless we embrace the good times and the bad times we will never reach our full potential. Our life's journey is like a spiritual ascent of Mt. Everest! Base camp is never our destination! Don't settle for that either! There are always unexpected twists and turns ahead of us and the occasional crevice! But take heart, the view from the top is far better than the view from down below.

Thank you for reading this, and I trust that you have read enough to cause you to press further into God. I trust that you will continue on you your journey of being a worshipper, and lover of God.

Finally, a story from Leslie Keegel.......

*A number of years ago, my 3 year old daughter came and sat on my knee and fell asleep. She had her ear close to my heart and she heard my heart beat. What is that? She asked, as she woke up? She had heard my heart beating inside me.*

*If you will draw close to my heart and keep your ear right where my heart is, you will hear my heart.*

*This is what intimacy is all about! Aligning our heart to his heart beat.*

# Conclusion

Involvement in a worship team is an honour, and it is much more that being able to play or sing songs. It is much more than being able to stand and perform in front of people. It requires a life given over to pursuing God's heart, in order that our lives become one of praise. Giving myself to the understanding of the power that praise and worship actually carries and giving my heart to the study of Biblical principles and their outworking in the Church. We must be willing to be students of others who have walked this path and then a father or mother to those who are following you.

We have a responsibility, that as we participate in this adventure, to give ourselves to pursuing God's heart and wisdom every step along the way. Also developing a living and active relationship with Holy Spirit, so that we can truly be:

God-focused
Christ-centred
Spirit-led

*As the deer pants for steams of water, so my should longs for you, O God.* Psalm 42:1

We must be willing to come again and again to drink at God's streams. Drinking this life-giving water will keep our lives satisfied forever.

# Psalm 139

## The Passion Translation

Lord, you know everything there is to know
about me.

You perceive every movement of my heart and
soul, and you understand my every thought
before it even enters my mind.

You are so intimately aware of me, Lord. You
read my heart like an open book
and you know all the words I'm about to speak
before I even start a sentence!
You know every step I will take before my
journey even begins.

You've gone into my future to prepare the way,
and in kindness you follow behind me to spare me
from the harm of my past. With your hand of love
upon my life, you impart a blessing to me.

This is just too wonderful, deep, and
incomprehensible! Your understanding of me
brings me wonder and strength.

Where could I go from your Spirit? Where could I run and hide from your face?

If I go up to heaven, you're there! If I go down to the realm of the dead, you're there too! If I fly with wings into the shining dawn, you're there! If I fly into the radiant sunset, you're there waiting!

Wherever I go, your hand will guide me; your strength will empower me. It's impossible to disappear from you or to ask the darkness to hide me, for your presence is everywhere, bringing light into my night.

There is no such thing as darkness with you. The night, to you, is as bright as the day; there's no difference between the two.

You formed my innermost being, shaping my delicate inside and my intricate outside, and wove them all together in my mother's womb. I thank you, God, for making me so mysteriously complex! Everything you do is marvelously breathtaking. It simply amazes me to think about it! How thoroughly you know me, Lord! You even formed every bone in my body when you created me in the secret place, carefully, skillfully shaping me from nothing to something.

You saw who you created me to be before I became me! Before I'd ever seen the light of day, the number of days you planned for me were already recorded in your book. Every single moment you are thinking of me! How precious and wonderful to consider that you cherish me constantly in your every thought!

O God, your desires toward me are more than the grains of sand on every shore! When I awake each morning, you're still with me.

O God, come and slay these bloodthirsty, murderous men! For I cry out, "Depart from me, you wicked ones!" See how they blaspheme your sacred name and lift up themselves against you, but all in vain!

Lord, can't you see how I despise those who despise you? For I grieve when I see them rise up against you. I have nothing but complete hatred and disgust for them. Your enemies shall be my enemies!

God, I invite your searching gaze into my heart. Examine me through and through;
find out everything that may be hidden within me. Put me to the test and sift through all my anxious cares. See if there is any path of pain I'm walking on, and lead me back to your glorious, everlasting ways – the path that brings me back to you.

# Available Music

## This Crown Belongs to You

Recorded at All Nations Church, this powerful album has 7 tracks on it as a collaboration between David Hadden and the other worship team members. It is available for download, streaming and on a physical disc.

# Breath of God

This instrumental album features David Hadden on keyboard and Paula Kasica on flute. It will carry you into the restful presence of God through the ten tracks, it is available for download and a physical disc.

# Living Under The Shadow of His Wing

This disc contains a selection of 17 songs penned by David Hadden. A compilation of recordings from long out-of-print albums. For copies contact David Hadden.

Contact Details

David Hadden
All Nations Centre Leicester
10 Frog Island
Leicester
LE3 5AG

Email: david@ancl.co.uk